The Workes of William Shakespeare

The Workes of William Shakespeare,

containing all his Comedies, Histories, and

Tragedies: Truely set forth, according to their first
ORIGINALL.

A flickbook by
Abram Games

PALLAS ATHENE

Abram Games and Shakespeare's Title Portrait

Abram Games is one of the most important and influential figures of 20th-century graphic design. Born Abraham Gamse in 1914, he was a child of immigrant parents living in the East End of London. He began his working life assisting his photographer father, finding work in a commercial art studio, before turning freelance. His career was changed by the war, when he became the Official War Poster Artist, designing 100 posters for the Army. These remain amongst the most recognisable and significant images of wartime Britain. His post-war career was hugely successful, thanks to winning the competition to design the emblem for the 1951 Festival of Britain. He designed posters, stamps and emblems for an array of important British institutions, commercial companies and charities, including

Opposite: Abram Games and his Shakespeare poster, 1988

Shell, British Airways, British Rail, London Transport, the Financial Times, Guinness and Penguin Books. He was also a painter and inventor. His personal philosophy of 'maximum meaning, minimum means' gave all his work a distinctive and memorable quality. Abram Games died in 1996; his work spanned six decades, creating a remarkable record of Britain's social history.

In 1975 Games was invited to design a poster for the Royal Shakespeare Theatre International Centenary Appeal. It proved to be very popular and sought after. The portrait motif was based on Martin Droeshout's copper engraving used as the frontispiece for the title page of the 1623 First Folio collection of Shakespeare's plays. The original poster was printed in the brick red of the RSC Theatre in Stratford upon Avon.

Games said, 'Shakespeare designed this himself! I pasted the titles of all thirty-seven plays, assembling them to follow the engraving. I started with *The Tempest* at the top and *All's Well that Ends Well* was the last piece of the jigsaw.' A consummate perfectionist, he was delighted that all the plays fitted exactly into his plan.

This is an unusual design for a Games poster: he was never keen on typography as he considered he was not technically proficient at it, nor patient enough. He invariably attempted to make posters with as little text as possible, trying as ever to convey the maximum meaning with the minimum means.

Two years after its publication, Games designed a flickbook, using the elements of his striking poster. He thought it would be a fun and useful educational tool. The prototype was found amongst the many papers he left at his death, eventually leading to the publication you have in your hands. 'All's Well That Ends Well'.

Naomi Games

To the Reader.

This Figure, that thou here seest put,
  It was for gentle Shakespeare cut;
Wherein the Grauer had a strife
  with Nature, to out-doo the life :
O, could he but haue drawne his wit
  As well in brasse, as he hath hit
Hisface ; the Print would then surpasse
  All, that vvas euer vvrit in brasse.
But, since he cannot, Reader, looke
  Not on his Picture, but his Booke.

                                  B. I.

Mr. WILLIAM
SHAKESPEARES
COMEDIES,
HISTORIES, &
TRAGEDIES.

Published according to the True Originall Copies.

LONDON
Printed by Isaac Iaggard, and Ed. Blount. 1623.

Note
by Abram Games

The 37 titles of Shakespeare's plays appear on the following pages in the order as printed in the First Folio of 1623 and ending with *Pericles Prince of Tyre,* which was not added to the collection until the Third Folio of 1664. The dates of writing and the order of the seven poems making up the complete works of William Shakespeare are those generally accepted by scholars.

This catalogue may be 'activated' by holding it in the left hand, your right thumb on the outside edge of the cover, bending it outwards and flicking the pages at a convenient rate.

[For this edition, we have completed the list of works with three plays often considered to be partly by Shakespeare, and two that are recorded but now lost, together with some poems and collections of mixed or disputed authorship. *Editors.*]

Opposite: A copy of the First Folio, open at the title page with Martin Droeshout's portrait

1611·12

The Tempest.

Caliban: Be not afear'd. The isle is full of noises,
  Sounds and sweet airs that give delight and hurt not.

Act III, scene 2

The Tempeſt.

1594·5

The two Gentlemen of Verona.

Duke: For long agone I have forgot to court;
Besides, the fashion of the time is changed.

Act III, scene 1

The Tempest.

The two Gentlemen of Uerona.

1598-9

The Merry Wiues of Windsor.

Pistol: He hath studied her will, and translated her will:
Out of honesty, into English.

Act I, scene 3

1602·4

Measure for Measure.

Isabella: Ignominy in ransom and free pardon
  Are of two houses; lawful mercy
  Is nothing kin to foul redemption.

Act II, scene 4

The Tempeſt.

The two Gentlemen of Verona.

Meaſure for
Meaſure.   The Merry Wiues of Windſor.

1593·4

The Comedie of Errors.

Antipholus of Syracuse: When the sun shines, let foolish gnats make sport
  But creep in crannies when he hides his beams,
  If you will jest with me, know my aspect
  And fashion your demeanour to my looks
  Or I will beat this method in your sconce.

Act II, scene 2

The Tempest.

The Comedie of Errors.

The two Gentlemen of Uerona.

Measure for
Measure.

The Merry Wiues of Windsor.

1598·9

Much adoe about Nothing.

Leonato: I pray thee, peace! I will be flesh and blood;
   For there was never yet philosopher
   That could endure toothache patiently.

Act V, scene 1

The Tempest.

The Comedie of Errors.

Much adoe about Nothing.

The two Gentlemen of Verona.

Measure for
Measure.

The Merry Wiues of Windsor.

1594·5

Loues Labour's lost.

Boyet: The tongues of mocking wenches are as keen
  As is the razor's edge invisible,
  Cutting a smaller hair than may be seen,
  Above the sense of sense.

Act V, scene 2

The Tempest.

The Comedie of Errors.

Much adoe about Nothing.

The two Gentlemen of Verona.

Loues Labour's loft.

Meafure for
Meafure.

The Merry Wiues of Windfor.

1595

A Midsommernights Dreame.

Oberon: I know a bank where the wild thyme blows,
Where oxlips and the nodding violet grows,
Quite overcanopied with luscious woodbine,
With sweet muskroses, and with eglantine.

Act II, scene 1

The Tempest.

The Comedie of Errors.

Much adoe about Nothing.

The two Gentlemen of Verona.

Loues Labour's lost.

Measure for Measure.

A Midsommer nights Dreame.
The Merry Wiues of Windsor.

1596 ·7

The Merchant of Venice.

Bassanio: Pray thee take pain
To allay with some cold drops of modesty
Thy skipping spirit, lest, through thy wild behaviour
I be misconstru'd in the place I go to
And lose my hopes.

Act II, scene 2

The Tempest.

The Comedie of Errors.

Much adoe about Nothing.

The two Gentlemen of Verona.

Loues Labour's lost.

The Merchant of Venice.
A Midsommer nights Dreame.
Measure for   The Merry Wiues of Windsor.
Measure.

1599 · 1600

As you like it.

Rosalind: No, faith, proud mistress, hope not after it;
   Tis not your inky brows, your black silk hair,
   Your bugle eyeballs, nor your cheek of cream
   That can entame my spirits to your worship.

Act III, scene 5

The Tempest.

The Comedie of Errors.

Much adoe about Nothing.

The two Gentlemen of Verona.

Loues Labour's lost.

As
you
like it.
  Measure for
  Measure.

The Merchant of Venice.
A Midsommer nights Dreame.
The Merry Wiues of Windsor.

1593·4

The
Taming of
the Shrew.

Katherina: I must dance bare-foot on her wedding day,
   And, for your love to her, lead apes in hell.

Act II, scene 1

The Tempest.

The Comedie of Errors.

Much adoe about Nothing.

The two Gentlemen of Verona.

Loues Labour's lost.

As you like it.
The Taming of the Shrew.
Measure for Measure.

The Merchant of Venice.
A Midsommernights Dreame.
The Merry Wiues of Windsor.

All's Well, that Ends Well.

Countess: God's mercy, maiden! does it curd thy blood
   To say I am thy mother? What's the matter
   That this distemper'd messenger of wet,
   The many-colour'd Iris, rounds thine eye?

Act I, scene 3

The Tempest.   All's Well, that Ends Well.
The Comedie of Errors.

Much adoe about Nothing.

The two Gentlemen of Verona.

Loues Labour's loft.

As
you   Taming of
like it.   the Shrew.   The Merchant of Venice.
Meafure for   A Midfommernights Dreame.
Meafure.   The Merry Wiues of Windfor.

1599 · 1600

Twelfe Night, or, What you will.

Viola: She never told her love
   But let concealment, like a worm i' the bud,
   Feed on her damask cheek: she pin'd in thought
   And with a green and yellow melancholy
   Sat like Patience on a monument,
   Smiling at grief.

Act II, scene 4

The Tempest.　　　　All's Well, that Ends Well.
　　　　　　　　　　　The Comedie of Errors.

Much adoe about Nothing.

Twelfe Night, or, What you will.

The two Gentlemen of Verona.

Loues Labour's lost.

As　　　The　　　
you　　Taming of　
like it.　the Shrew.　　The Merchant of Venice.
Meafure for　　A Midfommer nights Dreame.
Meafure.　　The Merry Wiues of Windfor.

1610·11

The Winters Tale.

Camillo: Prosperity's the very bond of love
  Whose fresh complexion and whose heart together
  Affliction alters.

Act IV, scene 3

The Tempest.   All's Well, that Ends Well.
The Winters Tale.   The Comedie of Errors.

Much adoe about Nothing.

Twelfe Night, or, What you will.

The two Gentlemen of Verona.

Loues Labour's lost.

As   The
you   Taming of
like it. the Shrew.   The Merchant of Venice.
Meafure for   A Midfommer nights Dreame.
Meafure.   The Merry Wiues of Windfor.

1596 ·7

The life
and death
of King John.

King John: There is so hot a summer in my bosom
   That all my bowels crumble up to dust;
   I am a scribbled form, drawn with a pen
   Upon a parchment, and against this fire
   Do I shrink up.

Act V, scene 7

The Tempeſt.   All's Well, that Ends Well.
The Winters Tale.   The Comedie of Errors.

Much adoe about Nothing.

Twelfe Night, or, What you will.

The two Gentlemen of Verona.

The   life
and   death
of King John.

Loues Labour's loſt.

As   The
you   Taming of
like it.   the Shrew.   The Merchant of Venice.
Meaſure for   A Midſommer nights Dreame.
Meaſure.   The Merry Wiues of Windſor.

1595

The life and death of Richard the fecond.

King Richard II: Now is this golden crown like a deep well;
   That owes two buckets filling one another;
   The empty ever dancing in the air,
   The other down, unseen and full of water:
   That bucket down and full of tears am I,
   Drinking my griefs whilst you mount up high.

Act IV, scene 1

The Tempeſt.　　　　All's Well, that Ends Well.
The Winters Tale.　　　The Comedie of Errors.

Much adoe about Nothing.

Twelfe Night, or, What you will.

The two Gentlemen of Uerona.

The　　　life
and　　　death
of King Iohn.

Loues Labour's loſt.

The　　As　　　The
life and　you　　Taming of
death of　like it.　the Shrew.
Richard the　Meaſure for　The Merchant of Venice.
Second.　　Meaſure.　A Midſommer nights Dreame.
　　　　　　　The Merry Wiues of Windſor.

1597·8

The First Part of King Henry the Fourth.

Prince Henry: I know you all, and will awhile uphold
  The unyoked humour of your idleness.

Act I, scene 2

The Tempest.
The Winters Tale.

Much adoe about Nothing.

Twelfe Night, or, What you will.

The two Gentlemen of Verona.

The
life
and   death
of King John.

Loues Labour's lost.

All's Well, that Ends Well.
The Comedie of Errors.
The First Part of
King Henry the
Fourth.

The
life and   As   The
you   Taming of
death of   like it.   the Shrew.
Richard the   Measure for
second.   Measure.

The Merchant of Venice.
A Midsommer nights Dreame.
The Merry Wiues of Windsor.

1597·8

The second Part of
King Henry the Fourth.

Archbishop of York: A habitation giddy and unsure,
  Hath he that buildeth on the vulgar heart.

Act I, scene 3

The Tempest.
The Winters Tale.

All's Well, that Ends Well.
The Comedie of Errors.
The First Part of
King Henry the
Fourth.

Much adoe about Nothing.

Twelfe Night, or, What you will.

The two Gentlemen of Verona.

The
and   life
death
of King John.

Loues Labour's lost.

The
life and
death of
Richard the
second.

As
you
like it.
Measure for
Measure.

The
Taming of
the Shrew.

The second Part of
King Henry the Fourth.
The Merchant of Venice.
A Midsommer nights Dreame.
The Merry Wiues of Windsor.

1598·9

The Life of Henry the Fift.

Chorus: The king is set from London, and the scene
 Is now transported, gentles, to Southampton;
 There is the playhouse now, there must you sit;
 And thence to France shall we convey you safe
 And bring you back, charming the narrow seas
 To give you gentle pass; for, if we may,
 We'll not offend one stomach with our play.

Act II, Prologue

The Tempest.
The Winters Tale.
The Life of Henry the Fift.
Much adoe about Nothing.

Twelfe Night, or, What you will.

The two Gentlemen of Verona.

The   life
and   death
of King Iohn.

Loues Labour's lost.

All's Well, that Ends Well.
The Comedie of Errors.
The First Part of
King Henry the
Fourth.

The As   The
life and you Taming of
death of like it. the Shrew.
Richard the Measure for
second.   Measure.

The second Part of
King Henry the Fourth.
The Merchant of Venice.
A Midsommernights Dreame.
The Merry Wiues of Windsor.

1589·91

The first Part of Henry the Sixt.

Warwick: But in these nice sharp quillets of the law,
Good faith, I am no wiser than a daw.

Act II, scene 4

The Tempest.
The Winters Tale.
The Life of Henry the Fift.
Much adoe about Nothing.

All's Well, that Ends Well.
The Comedie of Errors.
The First Part of
King Henry the
Fourth.

Twelfe Night, or, What you will.

The two Gentlemen of Verona.

The   life
and   death
of King Iohn.

Loues Labour's lost.

The
first
Part of Henry the Sixt.
The   As   The
life and   you   Taming of
death of   like it.   the Shrew.
Richard the Measure for
second.   Measure.

The second Part of
King Henry the Fourth.
The Merchant of Venice.
A Midsommer nights Dreame.
The Merry Wiues of Windsor.

1589·91

The second Part of Henry the Sixt.

Queen Margaret: Now 'tis the spring and weeds are shallow-rooted;
   Suffer them now and they'll o'ergrow the garden,
   And choke the herbs for want of husbandry.
   The reverent care I bear unto my lord
   Made me collect these dangers in the duke.

Act III, scene 1

The Tempest.
The Winters Tale.
The Life of Henry the Fift.
Much adoe about Nothing.

All's Well, that Ends Well.
The Comedie of Errors.
The First Part of
King Henry the
Fourth.

Twelfe Night, or, What you will.

The second Part of Henry the Sixt.
The two Gentlemen of Uerona.

The
and
of King Iohn.
life
death

Loues Labour's lost.

The
first
Part of Henry the Sixt.
The
life and
death of
Richard the
second.
As
you
like it.
Measure for
Measure.
The
Taming of
the Shrew.

The second Part of
King Henry the Fourth.
The Merchant of Venice.
A Midsommer nights Dreame.
The Merry Wiues of Windsor.

1589·91

The third Part of King Henry the Sixt.

Gloucester: I have no brother. I am like no brother;
  And this word 'love' which greybeards call divine
  Be resident in men like one another
  And not in me: I am myself alone.

Act V, scene 6

The Tempest.
The Winters Tale.
The Life of Henry the Fift.
Much adoe about Nothing.

All's Well, that Ends Well.
The Comedie of Errors.
The First Part
of King Henry the
Fourth.

Twelfe Night, or, What you will.

The second Part of Henry the Sixt.
The two Gentlemen of Verona.

The life
and death
of King John.

Loues Labour's lost.

The
first
Part of Henry the Sixt.
The Taming of the Shrew.
Measure for Measure.
The
life and
death of
Richard the
second.
As you like it.

The third Part of
King Henry the Sixt.
The second Part of
King Henry the Fourth.
The Merchant of Venice.
A Midsommernights Dreame.
The Merry Wiues of Windsor.

1592-3

The Life and Death of Richard the Third.

King Richard III: A horse, a horse, my kingdom for a horse!

Act V, scene 4

The Tempest.
The Winters Tale.
The Life of Henry the Fift.
Much adoe about Nothing.

All's Well, that Ends Well.
The Comedie of Errors.
The First Part of
King Henry the
Fourth.

Twelfe Night, or, What you will.

The second Part of Henry the Sixt.
The two Gentlemen of Verona.
The Life and Death of Richard
the Third.

The life
and death
of King John.

Loues Labour's lost.

The
first
Part of Henry the Sixt.
The As The
life and you Taming of
death of like it. the Shrew.
Richard the Measure for
second. Measure.

The third Part of
King Henry the Sixt.
The second Part of
King Henry the Fourth.
The Merchant of Venice.
A Midsommer nights Dreame.
The Merry Wiues of Windsor.

1612

The Life of King Henry the Eight.

I come no more to make you laugh; things now
That bear a weighty and a serious brow,
Sad high, and working, full of state and woe,
Such noble scenes as draw the eye to flow,
We now present.

Act I, Prologue

The Tempest.
The Winters Tale.
The Life of Henry the Fift.
Much adoe about Nothing.

All's Well, that Ends Well.
The Comedie of Errors.
The First Part of
King Henry the
Fourth.

Twelfe Night, or, What you will.

The second Part of Henry the Sixt.
The two Gentlemen of Verona.
The Life and Death of Richard
the Third.

The   life
and   death
of King John.

The   Loues Labour's lost.

Life of King
Henry the
Eight. The
first

The third Part of
King Henry the Sixt.
The second Part of
King Henry the Fourth.
The Merchant of Venice.
A Midsommer nights Dreame.
The Merry Wiues of Windsor.

The   Part of Henry the Sixt.
life and   As   The
death of   you   Taming of
Richard the like it.   the Shrew.
second.   Measure for
             Measure.

1601-2

The Tragedie of Troylus and Cressida.

Troylus: O, Cressida, but that the busy day
   Wak'd by the lark, hath rous'd the ribald crows,
   And dreaming night will hide our joys no longer:
   I would not from thee.

Act IV, scene 2

The Tempest.
The Winters Tale.
The Life of Henry the Fift.
Much adoe about Nothing.

All's Well, that Ends Well.
The Comedie of Errors.
The First Part of
King Henry the
Fourth.

Twelfe Night, or, What you will.

The second Part of Henry the Sixt.
The two Gentlemen of Verona.
The Life and Death of Richard
the Third.
The   life
and   death
of King John.

The   Loues Labour's loſt.

Life of King
Henry the
Eight. The
firſt

The   Part of Henry the Sixt.
life and   As   The
you   Taming of
death of   like it.   the Shrew.
Richard the   Meaſure for
ſecond.   Meaſure.

The third Part of
King Henry the Sixt.
The ſecond Part of
King Henry the Fourth.
The Merchant of Venice.
A Midſommernights Dreame.
The Merry Wiues of Windſor.
The Tragedie of Troylus and Creſſida.

1607·9

The Tragedie of Coriolanus.

Aufidius: I think he'll be to Rome
  As is the osprey to the fish, who takes it
  By sovereignty of nature.

Act IV, scene 7

The Tempest.
The Winters Tale.
The Life of Henry the Fift.
Much adoe about Nothing.

All's Well, that Ends Well.
The Comedie of Errors.
The First Part of
King Henry the
Fourth.

Twelfe Night, or, What you will.

The second Part of Henry the Sixt.
The two Gentlemen of Verona.
The Life and Death of Richard
the Third.

The Tragedie
of Coriolanus.

The   life
and   death
of King Iohn.

The   Loues Labour's lost.
Life of King
Henry the
Eight. The
first

The third Part of
King Henry the Sixt.
The second Part of
King Henry the Fourth.
The Merchant of Venice.
A Midsommer nights Dreame.
The Merry Wiues of Windsor.
The Tragedie of Troylus and Cressida.

The   Part of Henry the Sixt.
life and   As   The
death of   you   Taming of
Richard the like it. the Shrew.
second.   Measure for
           Measure.

1592-3

The Tragedie of Titus Andronicus.

Titus Andronicus: Come, and take choice of all my library,
  And so beguile thy sorrow.

Act IV, scene 1

The Tempest.
The Winters Tale.
The Life of Henry the Fift.
Much adoe about Nothing.

All's Well, that Ends Well.
The Comedie of Errors.
The First Part of
King Henry the
Fourth.

Twelfe Night, or, What you will.

The second Part of Henry the Sixt.
The two Gentlemen of Verona.
The Life and Death of Richard
the Third.

The Tragedie
of Coriolanus.

The
life
and death
of King John.

The Tragedie of
Titus Andronicus.
Loues Labour's lost.

Life of King
Henry the
Eight. The
first

The third Part of
King Henry the Sixt.
The second Part of
King Henry the Fourth.
The Merchant of Venice.
A Midsommer nights Dreame.
The Merry Wiues of Windsor.
The Tragedie of Troylus and Cressida.

The
life and
death of
Richard the
second.

Part of Henry the Sixt.
As The
you Taming of
like it. the Shrew.
Measure for
Measure.

1595

The Tragedie of Romeo and Juliet.

Capulet: Nay, sit, nay, sit, good cousin Capulet,
   For you and I are past our dancing days.

Act I, scene 5

The Tempest.
The Winters Tale.
The Life of Henry the Fift.
Much adoe about Nothing.

All's Well, that Ends Well.
The Comedie of Errors.
The First Part of
King Henry the
Fourth.

Twelfe Night, or, What you will.
The Tragedie of Romeo and Juliet.
The second Part of Henry the Sixt.
The two Gentlemen of Verona.
The Life and Death of Richard
the Third.

The Tragedie
of Coriolanus.

The life
and death
of King John.

The Tragedie of
Titus Andronicus.
Loues Labour's lost.

The
Life of King
Henry the
Eight. The
first

The third Part of
King Henry the Sixt.
The second Part of
King Henry the Fourth.
The Merchant of Venice.
A Midsommernights Dreame.
The Merry Wiues of Windsor.
The Tragedie of Troylus and Cressida.

The
life and
death of
Richard the
second.

Part of Henry the Sixt.
As
you
like it.

The
Taming of
the Shrew.
Measure for
Measure.

1604·5

Timon of Athens.

Timon: There's nothing level in our cursed natures
But direct villany. Therefore be abhorr'd
All feasts, societies and throngs of men!
His semblance, yea himself, Timon disdains;
Destruction fang mankind!

Act IV, scene 3

The Tempest.
The Winters Tale.
The Life of Henry the Fift.
Much adoe about Nothing.

All's Well, that Ends Well.
The Comedie of Errors.
The First Part of
King Henry the
Fourth.

Twelfe Night, or, What you will.
The Tragedie of Romeo and Iuliet.
The second Part of Henry the Sixt.
The two Gentlemen of Verona.
The Life and Death of Richard
the Third.

The Tragedie
of Coriolanus.

The
and
of King Iohn.
life
death

The Tragedie of
Titus Andronicus.
Loues Labours lost.
The

Life of King
Henry the
Eight. The
first

Timon of
Athens.

The third Part of
King Henry the Sixt.
The second Part of
King Henry the Fourth.
The Merchant of Venice.
A Midsommernights Dreame.
The Merry Wiues of Windsor.
The Tragedie of Troylus and Cressida.

The
life and
death of
Richard the
second.

Part of Henry the Sixt.
As
you
like it.
Measure for
Measure.
The
Taming of
the Shrew.

1599 · 1600

The Tragedie of Julius Cæsar.

Brutus: There is a tide in the affairs of men
  Which, taken at the flood, leads on to fortune.

Act IV, scene 3

The Tempest.
The Winters Tale.
The Life of Henry the Fift.
Much adoe about Nothing.
The Tragedie of Julius Cæsar.
Twelfe Night, or, What you will.
The Tragedie of Romeo and Juliet.
The second Part of Henry the Sixt.
The two Gentlemen of Verona.
The Life and Death of Richard
the Third.

The   life
and   death
of King John.   The Tragedie of
                     Titus Andronicus.
        The   Loues Labour's lost.

Life of King
Henry the
Eight. The   Timon of
first   Athens.

        Part of Henry the Sixt.
The   As   The
life and   you   Taming of
death of   like it.   the Shrew.
Richard the   Measure for
second.   Measure.

All's Well, that Ends Well.
The Comedie of Errors.
The First Part of
King Henry the
Fourth.

The Tragedie
of Coriolanus.

The third Part of
King Henry the Sixt.
The second Part of
King Henry the Fourth.
The Merchant of Venice.
A Midsommer nights Dreame.
The Merry Wiues of Windsor.
The Tragedie of Troylus and Cressida.

1604·6

The
Tragedie of Macbeth.

Macbeth: It is a tale
  Told by an idiot, full of sound and fury,
  Signifying nothing.

Act V, scene 5

The Tempest.
The Winters Tale.
The Life of Henry the Fift.
Much adoe about Nothing.
The Tragedie of Julius Cæsar
Twelfe Night, or, What you will.
The Tragedie of Romeo and Juliet.
The second Part of Henry the Sixt.
The two Gentlemen of Verona.
The Life and Death of Richard
the Third.

All's Well, that Ends Well.
The Comedie of Errors.
The First Part of
King Henry the
Fourth.

The Tragedie
of Coriolanus.

The   life
and   death
of King John.   The Tragedie of
Titus Andronicus.
The   Loues Labour's lost.

Life of King
Henry the
Eight. The   Timon of
first   Athens.

The third Part of
King Henry the Sixt.
The second Part of
King Henry the Fourth.

The   Part of Henry the Sixt.
life and   As   The
death of   you   Taming of
Richard the   like it.   the Shrew.
second. The   Measure for
Tragedie of Macbeth.   Measure.

The Merchant of Venice.
A Midsommer nights Dreame.
The Merry Wiues of Windsor.
The Tragedie of Troylus and Cressida.

1600·1

The Tragedie
of Hamlet.

Horatio: So shall you hear
   Of carnal, bloody and unnatural acts,
   Of accidental judgements, casual slaughters,
   Of deaths put on by cunning and forc'd cause,
   And, in this upshot, purposes mistook
   Fall'n on the inventors' heads.

Act V, scene 2

The Tempeſt.
The Winters Tale.
The Life of Henry the Fift.
Much adoe about Nothing.
The Tragedie of Iulius Cæſar.
Twelfe Night, or, What you will.
The Tragedie of Romeo and Iuliet.
The ſecond Part of Henry the Sixt.
The two Gentlemen of Verona.
The Life and Death of Richard
the Third.

All's Well, that Ends Well.
The Comedie of Errors.
The Firſt Part of
King Henry the
Fourth.

The Tragedie
of Coriolanus.

The
life
and death
of King Iohn.

The
life of King
Henry the
Eight. The
firſt

The Tragedie of
Titus Andronicus.
Loues Labour's loſt.
The Tragedie
of Hamlet.
Timon of
Athens.

Part of Henry the Sixt.
The
Taming of
the Shrew.
Meaſure for
Meaſure.

The
life and
death of
Richard the
ſecond. The
Tragedie of Macbeth.

As
you
like it.

The third Part of
King Henry the Sixt.
The ſecond Part of
King Henry the Fourth.
The Merchant of Venice.
A Midſommer nights Dreame.
The Merry Wiues of Windſor.
The Tragedie of Troylus and Creſſida.

1604·6

The Tragedie of King Lear.

King Lear: Ay, every inch a king.
  When I do stare, see how the subject quakes.

Act IV, scene 6

The Tempest.
The Winters Tale.
The Life of Henry the Fift.
Much adoe about Nothing.
The Tragedie of Julius Cæsar.
Twelfe Night, or, What you will.
The Tragedie of Romeo and Juliet.
The second Part of Henry the Sixt.
The two Gentlemen of Verona.
The Life and Death of Richard the Third.

All's Well, that Ends Well.
The Comedie of Errors.
The First Part of King Henry the Fourth.

The Tragedie of Coriolanus.
The Tragedie of King Lear.

The life and death of King John.

The Tragedie of Titus Andronicus.
Loues Labour's lost.
The Tragedie of Hamlet.
Timon of Athens.

Life of King Henry the Eight. The first Part of Henry the Sixt.

The As you like it. The Taming of the Shrew. Measure for Measure.

The life and death of Richard the second. The Tragedie of Macbeth.

The third Part of King Henry the Sixt.
The second Part of King Henry the Fourth.
The Merchant of Venice.
A Midsommernights Dreame.
The Merry Wiues of Windsor.
The Tragedie of Troylus and Cressida.

1602·4

The
Tragedie of Othello.

Iago: So will I turn her virtue into pitch
  And out of her own goodness make the net
  That shall enmesh them all.
                                        Act II, scene 3

The Tempeſt.
The Winters Tale.
The Life of Henry the Fift.
Much adoe about Nothing.
The Tragedie of Iulius Cæsar.
Twelfe Night, or, What you will.
The Tragedie of Romeo and Iuliet.
The ſecond Part of Henry the Sixt.
The two Gentlemen of Verona.
The Life and Death of Richard
the Third.

All's Well, that Ends Well.
The Comedie of Errors.
The Firſt Part of
King Henry the
Fourth.

The Tragedie
of Coriolanus.
The Tragedie
of King
Lear.

The
life
and death
of King Iohn.

The Tragedie of
Titus Andronicus.
The Loues Labour's loſt.
The Tragedie
of Hamlet.

Life of King
Henry the
Eight. The
firſt

Timon of
Athens.

The
Tragedie of Othello.
The third Part of
King Henry the Sixt.
The ſecond Part of
King Henry the Fourth.
The Merchant of Venice.
A Midſommernights Dreame.
The Merry Wiues of Windſor.
The Tragedie of Troylus and Creſsida.

The
life and
death of
Richard the
ſecond. The
Tragedie of Macbeth.

Part of Henry the Sixt.
As
you
like it.

The
Taming of
the Shrew.
Meaſure for
Meaſure.

1606·7

Anthony and Cleopatra.

Enobarbus: The poop was beaten gold,
   Purple the sails, and so perfumed that
   The winds were lovesick with them.

Act II, scene 2

The Tempest.
The Winters Tale.
The Life of Henry the Fift.
Much adoe about Nothing.
The Tragedie of Julius Cæsar.
Twelfe Night, or, What you will.
The Tragedie of Romeo and Juliet.
The second Part of Henry the Sixt.
The two Gentlemen of Verona.
The Life and Death of Richard
the Third.
The life
and death
of King John.
Anthony and
Cleopatra.The
Life of King
Henry the
Eight. The
first

The Tragedie of
Titus Andronicus.
Loues Labour's lost.
The Tragedie
of Hamlet.
Timon of
Athens.

Part of Henry the Sixt.
The
Taming of
the Shrew.
Measure for
Measure.

The
As
you
like it.

The
life and
death of
Richard the
second. The
Tragedie of Macbeth.

All's Well, that Ends Well.
The Comedie of Errors.
The First Part of
King Henry the
Fourth.

The Tragedie
of Coriolanus.
The Tragedie
of King
Lear.

The
Tragedie of Othello.
The third Part of
King Henry the Sixt.
The second Part of
King Henry the Fourth.
The Merchant of Venice.
A Midsommernights Dreame.
The Merry Wiues of Windsor.
The Tragedie of Troylus and Cressida.

1607-9

The Tragedie of Cymbeline.

Belarius: The art o' the court
  As hard to leave as keep, whose top to climb
  Is certain falling or so slippery that
  The fear's as bad as falling.

Act III, scene 3

The Tempeſt.
The Winters Tale.
The Life of Henry the Fiſt.
Much adoe about Nothing.
The Tragedie of Julius Cæsar.
Twelfe Night, or, What you will.
The Tragedie of Romeo and Juliet.
The ſecond Part of Henry the Sixt.
The two Gentlemen of Verona.
The Life and Death of Richard
the Third.

All's Well, that Ends Well.
The Comedie of Errors.
The Firſt Part of
King Henry the
Fourth. The
Tragedie of
Cymbeline.
The Tragedie
of Coriolanus.
The Tragedie
of King
Lear.

The   life
and   death
of King John.   The Tragedie of
Anthony and   Titus Andronicus.
Cleopatra. The   Loues Labour's loſt.
Life of King   The Tragedie
Henry the   of Hamlet.
Eight. The   Timon of
firſt   Athens.

The
Tragedie of Othello.
The third Part of
King Henry the Sixt.
The ſecond Part of
King Henry the Fourth.

The   Part of Henry the Sixt.
life and   As   The
death of   you   Taming of
Richard the like it. the Shrew.
ſecond. The   Meaſure for
Tragedie of Macbeth.   Meaſure.

The Merchant of Venice.
A Midſommer nights Dreame.
The Merry Wiues of Windſor.
The Tragedie of Troylus and Creſſida.

Pericles
Prince of Tyre.

Dionyza: Let not conscience
  Which is but cold, inflaming love i' the bosom
  Inflame too nicely; nor let pity, which
  Even women have cast off, melt thee, but be
  A soldier to thy purpose.

Act I, scene I

The Tempest.
The Winters Tale.
The Life of Henry the Fift.
Much adoe about Nothing.
The Tragedie of Julius Cæsar.
Twelfe Night, or, What you will.
The Tragedie of Romeo and Juliet.
The second Part of Henry the Sixt.
The two Gentlemen of Verona.
The Life and Death of Richard
the Third.

All's Well, that Ends Well.
The Comedie of Errors.
The First Part of
King Henry the
Fourth. The
Tragedie of
Cymbeline.
The Tragedie
of Coriolanus.
The Tragedie
of King
Lear.

The life Pericles
and death Prince of Tyre.
of King John. The Tragedie of
Anthony and Titus Andronicus.
Cleopatra. The Loues Labour's lost.
Life of King The Tragedie
Henry the of Hamlet.
Eight. The Timon of
first Athens.

The
Tragedie of Othello.
The third Part of
King Henry the Sixt.

Part of Henry the Sixt.
The As The
life and you Taming of
death of like it. the Shrew.
Richard the Measure for
second. The Measure.
Tragedie of Macbeth.

The second Part of
King Henry the Fourth.
The Merchant of Venice.
A Midsommer nights Dreame.
The Merry Wiues of Windsor.
The Tragedie of Troylus and Cressida.

1593

Venus and Adonis.

For, he being dead, with him is beauty slain;
And, beauty dead, black Chaos comes again.

Lines 1019-20

The Tempest.
The Winters Tale.
The Life of Henry the Fift.
Much adoe about Nothing.
The Tragedie of Iulius Cæsar.
Twelfe Night, or, What you will.
The Tragedie of Romeo and Iuliet.
The second Part of Henry the Sixt.
The two Gentlemen of Verona.
The Life and Death of Richard the Third.

All's Well, that Ends Well.
The Comedie of Errors.
The First Part of King Henry the Fourth. The Tragedie of Cymbeline.
The Tragedie of Coriolanus.
The Tragedie of King Lear.

The life and death of King Iohn. Anthony and Cleopatra. The Life of King Henry the Eight. The first

Pericles Prince of Tyre. The Tragedie of Titus Andronicus. Loues Labour's lost. The Tragedie of Hamlet. Timon of Athens.

The Tragedie of Othello.
The third Part of King Henry the Sixt.

The life and death of Richard the second. The Tragedie of Macbeth.

Part of Henry the Sixt. As you like it. The Taming of the Shrew. Measure for Measure. The

The second Part of King Henry the Fourth.
The Merchant of Venice.
A Midsommer nights Dreame.
The Merry Wiues of Windsor.
The Tragedie of Troylus and Cressida.

1594

The Rape of Lucrece.

Beauty itself doth of itself persuade
The eyes of men without an orator.

Lines 29-30

The Tempest.
The Winters Tale.
The Life of Henry the Fift.
Much adoe about Nothing.
The Tragedie of Julius Cæsar.
Twelfe Night, or, What you will.
The Tragedie of Romeo and Juliet.
The second Part of Henry the Sixt.
The two Gentlemen of Verona.
The Life and Death of Richard
the Third.

All's Well, that Ends Well.
The Comedie of Errors.
The First Part of
King Henry the
Fourth.   The
Tragedie of
Cymbeline.
The Tragedie
of Coriolanus.
The Tragedie
of King
Lear.

The
life
and   death   Pericles
of King John.   Prince   of Tyre.
Anthony and   The Tragedie of
Cleopatra.The   Titus Andronicus.
Life of King   Loues Labour's lost.
Henry the   The Tragedie
Eight. The   of Hamlet.
first   Timon of
Athens.

The
Tragedie of Othello.
The third Part of
King Henry the Sixt.
The second Part of
Part of Henry the Sixt.   King Henry the Fourth.
The   The Merchant of Venice.
The   As   Taming of   A Midsommer nights Dreame.
life and   you   the Shrew.   The Merry Wiues of Windsor.
death of   like it.   Measure for   The Tragedie of Troylus and Cressida.
Richard the   Measure.
second.   The
Tragedie of Macbeth.

1601

The Phoenix and the Turtle.

So they lov'd, as love in twain
Had the essence but in one;
Two distincts, division none:
Number there in love was slain.

Lines 25-28

The Tempeſt.
The Winters Tale.
The Life of Henry the Fiſt.
Much adoe about Nothing.
The Tragedie of Iulius Cæsar.
Twelfe Night, or, What you will.
The Tragedie of Romeo and Iuliet.
The ſecond Part of Henry the Sixt.
The two Gentlemen of Verona.
The Life and Death of Richard
the Third.

All's Well, that Ends Well.
The Comedie of Errors.
The Firſt Part of
King Henry the
Fourth.   The
Tragedie of
Cymbeline.
The Tragedie
of Coriolanus.
The Tragedie
of King
Lear.

The   life   Pericles
and   death Prince   of Tyre.
of King Iohn.   The Tragedie of
Anthony and   Titus Andronicus.
Cleopatra. The Loues Labour's loſt.
Life of King   The Tragedie
Henry the   of Hamlet.
Eight. The   Timon   of
firſt   Athens.

The
Tragedie of Othello.
The third Part of
King Henry the Sixt.
The ſecond Part of
King Henry the Fourth.
The Merchant of Venice.

Part of Henry the Sixt.
The   As   The
life and you   Taming of
death of like it. the Shrew.
Richard the   Measure for
ſecond. The   Measure.
Tragedie of Macbeth.

A Midſommernights Dreame.
The Merry Wiues of Windsor.
The Tragedie of Troylus and Creſsida.

1609

Sonnets.

When to the sessions of sweet silent thought
I summon up remembrance of things past,
I sigh the lack of many a thing I sought
And with old woes new wail my dear time's waste.

Sonnet 30, lines 1-4

The Tempest.
The Winters Tale.
The Life of Henry the Fift.
Much adoe about Nothing.
The Tragedie of Iulius Cæsar.
Twelfe Night, or, What you will.
The Tragedie of Romeo and Iuliet.
The second Part of Henry the Sixt.
The two Gentlemen of Verona.
The Life and Death of Richard the Third.

All's Well, that Ends Well.
The Comedie of Errors.
The First Part of King Henry the Fourth. The Tragedie of Cymbeline.
The Tragedie of Coriolanus.
The Tragedie of King Lear.

The life and death of King Iohn.
Pericles Prince of Tyre.
Anthony and Cleopatra. The Life of King Henry the Eight. The first

The Tragedie of Titus Andronicus.
Loues Labour's lost.
The Tragedie of Hamlet.
Timon of Athens.

The Tragedie of Othello.
The third Part of King Henry the Sixt.
The second Part of King Henry the Fourth.

Part of Henry the Sixt.
The life and death of Richard the second. The Tragedie of Macbeth.

As you like it.
The Taming of the Shrew.
Measure for Measure.

The Merchant of Venice.
A Midsommer nights Dreame.
The Merry Wiues of Windsor.
The Tragedie of Troylus and Cressida.

1592

Sir Thomas More.

Sir Thomas More: Imagine that you see the wretched strangers,
  Their babies at their backs and their poor luggage,
  Plodding to the ports and coasts for transportation,
  And that you sit as kings in your desires

Act II, scene 4

Play possibly by Chettle, Dekker, Heywood and Shakespeare

The Tempest.
The Winters Tale.
The Life of Henry the Fift.
Much adoe about Nothing.
The Tragedie of Iulius Cæsar.
Twelfe Night, or, What you will.
The Tragedie of Romeo and Iuliet.
The second Part of Henry the Sixt.
The two Gentlemen of Verona.
The Life and Death of Richard
the Third.

All's Well, that Ends Well.
The Comedie of Errors.
The First Part of
King Henry the
Fourth. The
Tragedie of
Cymbeline.
The Tragedie
of Coriolanus.
The Tragedie
of King
Lear.

The life Pericles
and death Prince of Tyre.
of King Iohn. The Tragedie of
Anthony and Titus Andronicus.
Cleopatra. The Loues Labour's lost.
Life of King The Tragedie
Henry the of Hamlet.
Eight. The Timon of
first Athens.

The
Tragedie of Othello.
The third Part of
King Henry the Sixt.
The second Part of
King Henry the Fourth.
The Merchant of Venice.
A Midsommernights Dreame.
The Merry Wiues of Windsor.
The Tragedie of Troylus and Cressida.

Part of Henry the Sixt.
The life and As The
death of you Taming of
Richard the like it. the Shrew.
second. The Measure for
Tragedie of Macbeth. Measure.

1596

Edward the Third.

Warwick: Dark night seems darker by the lightning flash;
  Lilies, that fester, smell far worse than weeds;
  And every glory that inclines to sin,
  The same is treble by the opposite.

Act II, scene I

Play possibly by Shakespeare with Thomas Kyd

The Tempest.
The Winters Tale.
The Life of Henry the Fift.
Much adoe about Nothing.
The Tragedie of Iulius Cæsar.
Twelfe Night, or, What you will.
The Tragedie of Romeo and Iuliet.
The second Part of Henry the Sixt.
The two Gentlemen of Verona.
The Life and Death of Richard
the Third.

All's Well, that Ends Well.
The Comedie of Errors.
The First Part of
King Henry the
Fourth.   The
Tragedie of
Cymbeline.
The Tragedie
of Coriolanus.
The Tragedie
of King
Lear.

The
life
and   death
of King Iohn.
Anthony and
Cleopatra. The
Life of King
Henry the
Eight. The
first

Pericles
Prince   of Tyre.
The Tragedie of
Titus Andronicus.
Loues Labour's lost.
The Tragedie
of Hamlet.
Timon of
Athens.

The
Tragedie of Othello.
The third Part of
King Henry the Sixt.
The second Part of
King Henry the Fourth.
The Merchant of Venice.
A Midsommer nights Dreame.
The Merry Wiues of Windsor.
The Tragedie of Troylus and Cressida.

Part of Henry the Sixt.
The   As
life and   you
death of   like it.
Richard the   Measure for
second.   The   Measure.
Tragedie of Macbeth.

The
Taming of
the Shrew.

1598

Loues Labour's won.

Benedick: I would I could find in my heart that I had not a hard heart, for truly I love none.

Much Ado about Nothing, Act I, scene 1

Lost play by Shakespeare or possibly alternative recorded name for *Much Ado*

The Tempest.
The Winters Tale.
The Life of Henry the Fift.
Much adoe about Nothing.
The Tragedie of Julius Cæsar.
Twelfe Night, or, What you will.
The Tragedie of Romeo and Iuliet.
The second Part of Henry the Sixt.
The two Gentlemen of Verona.
The Life and Death of Richard
the Third.

All's Well, that Ends Well.
The Comedie of Errors.
The First Part of
King Henry the
Fourth. The
Tragedie of
Cymbeline.
The Tragedie
of Coriolanus.
The Tragedie
of King
Lear.

The life Pericles
and death Prince of Tyre.
of King John. The Tragedie of
Anthony and Titus Andronicus.
Cleopatra. The Loues Labour's lost.
Life of King The Tragedie
Henry the of Hamlet.
Eight. The Timon of
first Athens.

The
Part of Henry the Sixt.
The life and As The
death of you Taming of
Richard the like it the Shrew.
second. The Measure for
Tragedie of Macbeth. Measure.

The
Tragedie of Othello.
The third Part of
King Henry the Sixt.
The second Part of
King Henry the Fourth.
The Merchant of Venice.
A Midsommernights Dreame.
The Merry Wiues of Windsor.
The Tragedie of Troylus and Cressida.

1613

The two Noble Kinsmen.

Third Queen: He that will all the treasure know o'th' earth
   Must know the centre too; he that will fish
   For my least minnow, let him lead his line
   To catch one at my heart.

Act I, scene 1

Play possibly by Shakespeare with John Fletcher

The Tempest.
The Winters Tale.
The Life of Henry the Fift.
Much adoe about Nothing.
The Tragedie of Julius Cæsar.
Twelfe Night, or, What you will.
The Tragedie of Romeo and Juliet.
The second Part of Henry the Sixt.
The two Gentlemen of Verona.
The Life and Death of Richard
the Third.

All's Well, that Endr Well.
The Comedie of Errors.
The First Part of
King Henry the
Fourth. The
Tragedie of
Cymbeline.
The Tragedie
of Coriolanus.
The Tragedie
of King
Lear.

The
life
and
death
of King John.
Anthony and
Cleopatra. The
Life of King
Henry the
Eight, The
first

Pericles
Prince of Tyre.
The Tragedie of
Titus Andronicus.
Loues Labour's lost.
The Tragedie
of Hamlet.
Timon of
Athens.

The
Tragedie of Othello.
The third Part of
King Henry the Sixt.
The second Part of
King Henry the Fourth.
The Merchant of Venice.
A Midsommernights Dreame.
The Merry Wiues of Windsor.
The Tragedie of Troylus and Cressida.

Part of Henry the Sixt.
As   The
you   Taming of
like it   the Shrew.
Measure for
Measure.

life and
death of
Richard the
second. The
Tragedie of Macbeth.

1613

Cardenio.

Violenta (singing): Woods, rocks and mountains and ye desert places
  Where naught but bitter cold and hunger dwells,
  Hear a poor maid's last will, killed with disgraces.

Act IV, scene 3

Lost play possibly by Shakespeare with John Fletcher

The Tempest.
The Winters Tale.
The Life of Henry the Fift.
Much adoe about Nothing.
The Tragedie of Julius Cæsar.
Twelfe Night, or, What you will.
The Tragedie of Romeo and Juliet.
The second Part of Henry the Sixt.
The two Gentlemen of Verona.
The Life and Death of Richard the Third.

The life and death of King John. Anthony and Cleopatra. The Life of King Henry the Eight. The first

Pericles Prince of Tyre. The Tragedie of Titus Andronicus. Loues Labour's lost. The Tragedie of Hamlet. Timon of Athens.

All's Well, that Ends Well.
The Comedie of Errors.
The First Part of King Henry the Fourth. The Tragedie of Cymbeline.
The Tragedie of Coriolanus.
The Tragedie of King Lear.

The Tragedie of Othello.
The third Part of King Henry the Sixt.
The second Part of King Henry the Fourth.
The Merchant of Venice.
A Midsommer nights Dreame.
The Merry Wiues of Windsor.
The Tragedie of Troylus and Cressida.

Part of Henry the Sixt. The life and death of Richard the second. The Tragedie of Macbeth.

As you like it. The Taming of the Shrew. Measure for Measure.

1599

The Passionate Pilgrim.

If love make me forsworn, how shall I swear to love?
O, never faith could hold, if not to beauty vowed:
Though to myself forsworn, to thee I'll constant prove;
Those thoughts, to me like oaks, to thee like osiers bowed.

Sonnet 5, lines 1-4

Anthology published as by Shakespeare, but mostly containing
works by others

The Tempest.
The Winters Tale.
The Life of Henry the Fift.
Much adoe about Nothing.
The Tragedie of Julius Cæsar.
Twelfe Night, or, What you will.
The Tragedie of Romeo and Juliet.
The second Part of Henry the Sixt.
The two Gentlemen of Verona.
The Life and Death of Richard the Third.

All's Well, that Ends Well.
The Comedie of Errors.
The First Part of King Henry the Fourth. The Tragedie of Cymbeline. The Tragedie of Coriolanus. The Tragedie of King Lear.

Pericles Prince of Tire.
The life and death of King John. Anthony and Cleopatra. The Life of King Henry the Eight. The first Part of Henry the Sixt.

The Tragedie of Titus Andronicus. Loues Labour's lost. The Tragedie of Hamlet. Timen of Athens.

The Tragedie of Othello. The third Part of King Henry the Sixt.

The Part of Henry the Sixt. As you like it. The Taming of the Shrew. Measure for Measure.

The life and death of Richard the second. The Tragedie of Macbeth.

The second Part of King Henry the Fourth. The Merchant of Venice. A Midsommer nights Dreame. The Merry Wiues of Windsor. The Tragedie of Troylus and Cressida.

1609

Sonnets to sundry Notes of Musik.

On a day (alack the day!)
Love, whose month was ever May,
Spied a blossom passing fair,
Playing in the wanton air.

No. 17, lines 1-4

Poems published with The Passionate Pilgrim,
with one accepted as being by Shakespeare

The Tempest.
The Winters Tale.
The Life of Henry the Fift.
Much adoe about Nothing.
The Tragedie of Julius Cæsar.
Twelfe Night, or, What you will.
The Tragedie of Romeo and Juliet.
The second Part of Henry the Sixt.
The two Gentlemen of Verona.
The Life and Death of Richard the Third.

All's Well, that Ends Well.
The Comedie of Errors.
The First Part of King Henry the Fourth. The Tragedie of Cymbeline. The Tragedie of Coriolanus. The Tragedie of King Lear.

The life and death of King John. Anthony and Cleopatra. The Life of King Henry the Eight. The first

Pericles Prince of Tyre. The Tragedie of Titus Andronicus. Loues Labour's lost. The Tragedie of Hamlet. Timon of Athens.

The Part of Henry the Sixt. The Taming of the Shrew. Measure for Measure.

The life and death of Richard the second. The Tragedie of Macbeth.

The Tragedie of Othello. The third Part of King Henry the Sixt. The second Part of King Henry the Fourth. The Merchant of Venice. A Midsommer nights Dreame. The Merry Wiues of Windsor. The Tragedie of Troylus and Cressida.

1599

To the Queen.

So, most mighty Queen we pray,
Like the dial day by day

You may lead the seasons on,
Making new when old are gone.

Lines 5-8

Poem possibly by Shakespeare, written for
a performance of As You Like It

The Tempest.
The Winters Tale.
The Life of Henry the Fift.
Much adoe about Nothing.
The Tragedie of Julius Cæsar.
Twelfe Night, or, What you will.
The Tragedie of Romeo and Juliet.
The ſecond Part of Henry the Sixt.
The two Gentlemen of Verona.
The Life and Death of Richard the Third.

All's Well, that Ends Well.
The Comedie of Errors.
The First Part of King Henry the Fourth.
The Tragedie of Cymbeline.
The Tragedie of Coriolanus.
The Tragedie of King Lear.

The life and death of King John. The Tragedie of Anthony and Cleopatra. The Life of King Henry the Eight. The first

Pericles Prince of Tyre. The Tragedie of Titus Andronicus. Loues Labour's lost. The Tragedie of Hamlet. The Timon of Athens.

The Tragedie of Othello.
The third Part of King Henry the Sixt.
The ſecond Part of King Henry the Fourth.
The Merchant of Venice.

Part of Henry the Sixt. The life and death of Richard the Second. The Tragedie of Macbeth.

The Taming of the Shrew. Measure for Measure. A Midsommer nights Dreame.
The Merry Wiues of Windsor.
The Tragedie of Troylus and Cressida.

1609

A Louer's Complaint.

I might as yet have been a spreading flower,
Fresh to myself, if I had self-applied
Love to myself and to no love beside.

Lines 75-77
Poem published with the Sonnets, but of disputed authorship